THE Happy DIET

1st Edition eBook, published by Tamara Armstrong © at **Smashwords**, 2016
1st Edition paperback, published by Tamara Armstrong © 2017

ISBN: 978 1 9997164 0 0

Book designed and printed in the UK by **Tamara Armstrong**

THE *Happy* DIET

BY TAMARA ARMSTRONG   NOT
DR.
TAMARA

•LONDON•

CONTENTS

CONTENTS

For my Grams,
thank you for always
believing in me.

THE HAPPY DIET

Welcome to The Happy Diet. I am Tamara Armstrong. There are no fancy letters after my name and none in front either. I am NOT a doctor. I don't prescribe anything that your doctor does, just all the things that they should. This is a relatively small book but as with all things, greatness can come from the smallest of things so do not judge this book by its page numbers, or lack of. As easily, gently and quickly as I can, I want to help you find your 'happy' and as it's all quite simple, I don't need a 6,000 page book to explain it. At the end of this diet I want you to have the type of happiness that keeps you warm at night. The type of happiness that if aliens came and destroyed our planet and only you survived, you would be wandering the earth alone and still be happy.

IT'S ALL IN YOUR HEAD

The funny thing with happiness is, even though its the thing most vital to our survival, we often misunderstand what it actually is. The most important thing that we need to realise is that happiness not actually a 'thing', it's a state of being. This state of 'being' may not come naturally to all because of many surrounding factors but it can come more easily with the right lifestyle choices. Yes you can buy things that will make you happy, but bought happiness in the form of material things tends to not be real and doesn't ever last long. What we all deserve is to be as happy as children. Children are great examples of how to be happy as they live in a constant state of awe at most things. Living in this state means the things we view as 'normal' and 'everyday' are full of magic and wonder to most children. It's a bit of this magic that I want to help you to recapture.

I do not mess around in this book, it's short, sharp and very concise. If you want to learn to live on the brighter side of life then this is the book for you. Yes, you will still encounter hiccups at times but that is all part of life. What's important is how you deal with those hiccups. The advice in this book is designed to give the best possible quality of life by providing you with tools, habits and routines to better yourself, so even when bad things do happen you are better equipped to deal with them and you may even be able to find a way to use them to your advantage.

IT'S THE LITTLE THINGS

How we appreciate even the simplest of things can have a huge impact on our happiness and our moods in general. Next time you go for a walk take time to stop and admire how the trees and flowers grow so beautifully. Take a deep look into the stem of a flower, notice the colours, the symmetry, the mathematical genius that has occured. You could wander to your local food market and smell all the fresh fruit, close your eyes and really breathe in that fragrant air. Go for a midnight stroll and have a good look at the moon and the stars. If things ever get too much, I always go and look at the stars. We live in such a vast universe that its sometimes easy to forget that in the grand scheme of things our problems are nothing, we are barely a dot in existence. Now this may sound silly compared to fresh flowers and the stars but one thing I truly admire is the roads and yes, I do mean the roads we drive on. Whilst you could choose to moan about traffic jams and potholes, I actually think wow. Just WOW. Have you ever really thought about all the time and energy that went into building the roads we drive on so thoughtlessly?

Just think, a few hundred years ago roads as we know them did not even exist. Someone's Great Grandad built them and just think about that for a second. Humans built all these roads and all these roads go to so many places. It's sounds stupid to think so deeply about roads, but the more you do think, the more you start to see the real beauty of them. It truly amazes me when I'm driving just how far the roads go and how they go everywhere. I am genuinley grateful for the roads and the endless places we are able to go on them. I really think it's all so very clever and the attitude I have towards roads and my life in general is why I think I have a happier existence. Finding the beauty in all things is a bit of an art but, once you master it, it will make your life truly worth living.

IT'S STILL ALL IN YOUR HEAD

Often happiness is not a result of what is happening in our life it's more a result of what we THINK OF what is happening that really affects us. Happy people tend to try and look for the good in the situation even if it seems hopeless. The happiest people will remain positive and try to figure out the solution to their problem or situation. A wise person knows nothing bad happens without a lesson and a reason. If you can turn a bad situation into an opportunity for growth, that's when you are winning at life. You see its not necessarily about whether the glass is half empty or even half full, what it's about is being grateful for the fact you have a glass!

SOON YOU SHALL START YOUR NEW LIFE.....

OK, so about this diet and it's rules. This diet is serious and will help put you on a path to a happier life if followed correctly BUT, and this is a big BUT, this diet is not to be approached with so much seriousness that it is then to the detriment of your happiness. That means if something is to difficult for you or you don't feel quite like it one day or any day, then (and to quote one of my favourite books) F**K IT! Don't do it as this diet is not about stress, in fact it's about entirely the opposite. At the end of this diet I want you to feel like you have been kissed by a thousand unicorns and danced under a million rainbows. A slightly trippy exaggeration, but I do want you your soul to be warm and your heart to happy.

THE HAPPY DIET

This diet lasts for a month. That's four tiny weeks. If done properly and mindfully, it will be enough to start to change your life for the better. The new habits you adopt whilst on this diet will help to happily carry you through the rest of your life. You don't have to continue with them all BUT, the parts of this diet that make your whole being glow, those are the parts that, if you considered doing for life, you would probably be one of the happiest humans alive.

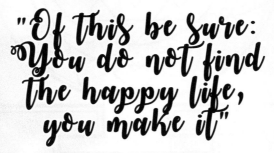

"Of this be sure:
You do not find
the happy life,
you make it"

THOMAS S MONSON

week 1

THE HAPPY DIET

....

"take care of your body,
it's the only place
you have to live"

JIM ROHN

EAT S*#T AND YOU WILL PROBABLY DIE

Put simply, the most crucial change you will make to your life for the better will be what you use to fuel you. We hear it time and again and it's a cliché but if you put the wrong petrol in your car-it will break down. A HUGE part of our mood is attributed to the food that we eat as our body converts whatever we eat into energy. If our diet is bad and lacking in nutrients and vitamins or we are eating things that are detrimental to our insides and well-being, then WE are going to break down. If your diet is mainly plant based and full of goodness then you can skip this bit and use this week to organise a party to celebrate your amazing choices! But if it's not then you really need to start cutting down on the amount of processed and chemically laden products you eat and drink. MSG, GMO's, Aspartame, food colourings, they are all a toxic chemical storm just waiting to try and kill you. Aspartame is an artificial sweetener used in most things labelled 'sugar free' and is banned in the rest of the EU in all childrens products due to it's side effects being so harmful. Shockingly aspartame can be linked with everything from depression to brain lesions! MSG (monosodium glutamate) is a flavour enhancer that is used in a lot of foods and when researchers fed it to animal test subjects it was found to cause gross obesity. Did you also know after feeding rats genetically modified food (GMO'S) they contracted an alarmingly high amount of diseases and tumors. Worryingly in October of 2015 The WHO (The World Health Organisation) declared all processed meat a type 1 carcinogen, meaning things like sausages and chicken nuggets are now placed in the same toxic category as tobacco smoking and asbestos! I think if you did some of your own research about certain foods we consider 'normal' you would be genuinley shocked. Whilst this is not the place to go into it, it is important to think about researching a little as it is vital to know what you are putting into yourself.

For the next four weeks we are going to journey together through a healthier eating regime.

Unfortunately, for some of you who eat meat you may not like what I say next, so brace yourself. Meat is not just 'meat'. It was once an animal with a set of eyes, ears, a heart, a soul and feelings just like you and me. There is no difference between a dog, a cat and a cow, only that somewhere along the line we started calling cows burgers and pigs bacon. I do not accept that pigs and cows are any different to cats and dogs, or even us. ALL 'beings' have a soul whether human or animal and there is not one ounce of happiness to be gained by eating any kind of meat, trust me. You don't just eat 'meat' when you have a burger or a steak, you are consuming an energy source that's made from death, fear, sadness, pain and let's not forget whatever medication/growth hormones the animals have been fed on to grow. I honestly believe you cannot be truly happy if you are eating meat, so for this week and the following 3 weeks, please just try and bare with me and follow this diet. All that you need to do this week is stop your intake of red meat. Have chicken and fish by all means, but in week one, you need to cut out ALL red meat. It is important to note that in October 2015 The World Health Organisation declared all red meat a type 2 carcinogen, meaning it might give you cancer. That's quite worrying and one of the main reasons you should try and eliminate it from your diet.

If you are worried that you will turn into a leaf munching hippy, rest assured that you are not the only one. More and more people are switching to a plant based diet and discovering there are numerous health benefits to be had from going vegan. In 1931 a German doctor named Otto Warburg was awarded the Nobel Peace prize for discovering that cancer was caused by a lack of oxygen in the body. Everything green and leafy is packed full of oxygen and apart from using oxygen therapy, eating a plant based diet is the fastest, easiest and healthiest way to get o2 pumping around your body and avoid cancer.

"Let food be Thy Medicine"

HIPPOCRATES

WATER YOURSELF

We are like flowers, dried, shrivelled up flowers unfortunately for most, but flowers nonetheless and we need constant watering. We humans are roughly 60% water but barely any of us get enough of the stuff. Being even slightly dehydrated can be the start of serious problems such as fatigue, migraines, loss of concentration and dry skin. Severe dehydration can cause all sorts of long term problems and it can even lead to death so it really is VITAL that we get enough water. This week you need to set up 5-6 daily alarms to go off to remind you to drink at least 1 glass of water every time it goes off.

A GOOD START TO THE DAY

The best (and I believe necessary) start to everyday is a large glass of room temperature water with some freshly squeezed lemon, followed by a super healthy vitamin and nutrient dense drink. We are very dehydrated when we wake up and a great way to rehydrate your beautiful body with a load of nutrients is homemade smoothies or freshly pressed juices with added extras such as Wild Blue Green Algae powder and/or chia seeds. Smoothies are so easy to make and there are plenty of recipes on the internet to try. Consider going to your local market to buy fresh, loose fruit and veg, it will be a lot cheaper, more sustainable and you will feel happier. You can spend the money that you saved from not eating red meat!

WHAT TO AVOID

Try not to drink anything labelled 'sugar free' or 'diet'. Ironically it's these products that are filled with chemicals more harmful than the ones they claiming to replace. Sugar is highly toxic and VERY bad for you but these artificial sweeteners (like aspartame) are 100 x worse. I'd rather lick snot off a stranger than drink a diet cola.

CUTTING DOWN TV

Ok, so do you really want to change your life and be happier? Try to stop watching so much television. Seriously, TV is more dangerous than Bruce Banner in a china shop. It will be a harsh truth for some, but those who it is hardest for are the ones who probably need to cut down the most. Think about what you are 'tuning' into. Think about what these programmes are 'programming' you with. The television, and why it's bad for you, is another book in itself BUT understand this: the television and its 'programmes' are not here to serve you, your higher consciousness or your happiness at all. I am not suggesting you never watch anything again as that would be ridiculous, what I am saying is things like reality TV and the news has to go. Especially the news. The evening news tends to be scarier than most horror films these days and if you are as sensitive as I am then you will be emotionally affected by what you see on a day to day basis. It can really create a feeling of dread in you and as our emotions are ultimately what create our universal experience, it's vital we have more good feelings than bad. I do not believe it is productive to watch the news because of the amount of fear and anxiety it can instill in us. We cannot do anything about the situation being shown and often what is shown is either of a biased nature or has an ulterior motive, so it makes little sense to watch it. Reality TV is another complete waste of our time and ironically most 'reality' TV is often far from any of our actual realities. We would probably all be happier if we just focused on our own reality and well-being. So the next step in week 1 of 'The Happy Diet' is a limit on television to 1 hour a day. That may not seem like much but remember no-one is paying you to watch TV and you are not getting any wiser by watching it.

At the end of this book there is a list
of other suggested reading and it would be good to try to get 1 or 2 of
the books mentioned to read whilst you are fasting from television.
Reading is not only a great way to expand your mind but a wonderful
way to relax too.

LESS FACE, MORE BOOKS

Social media is another (bad) habit that you should not engage in for
more than an hour a day. These things can be damaging to our well-
being. Constantly seeing others live a life we perceive to be perfect life
may not be productive to our own lives. Looking at happy couples
when you are alone can be soul destroying and seeing people flashing
cash if you can barely afford to eat won't inspire you, it will just depress
you. Remember, people that are having a genuinely good time rarely
find time to share it all on social media, most of it is a front to either
sell you something or a front to sell you something (no that's not a
typo). However most people don't get that its all just a sales pitch and
their desire for what they think is making other people happy is what
keeps them unhappy.
The irony is an overactive use of social media can actually impair our
ability to communicate with people in real life. People have become so
used to hiding behind a screen where they can pretend to be whatever
they like, that when it comes to real life communication, some people
struggle. That's not normal, healthy or going to make you happy, so try
to keep social networking to 1 hour a day.

THE HAPPY DIET WEEK 1 SUMMARY:

- No more than 1 hour of TV and 1 hour of social networking a day

- Start reading from the suggested book list or books of your choice

- WATER YOURSELF! Set alarms to go off at least 5-6 times a day and start EVERY day with 300ml at least of room temperature water.

- Invent a SUPER drink to have every morning

- No red meat

- Cut down all artificial/chemical laden foods and diet foods/drinks

ADDED HAPPY:

Adding a slice of organic unwaxed lemon to the water you drink throughout the day can have such a massive impact on you. Freshly squeezed lemon and the oils from the skin will help with detoxing, weight loss, skin problems and most importantly-YOUR MOOD. Lemon is natural antibacterial, antifungal, antidepressant (it's very high in potassium) and anti-inflammatory. It helps to strengthen your immune system and helps to keep your body alkalised. Apart from the fact it tastes better that plain water, drinking lemon water is so beneficial that you'd be a lemon if you didn't drink it! *Use a straw to drink lemon water to avoid acid erosion on your teeth.

THE HAPPY DIET

·····································

"if you cannot do great things, do small things in a great way"

NAPOLEON HILL

YOGA

Week 2 is all about getting our frequency right. Whether we like it or not, exercise in some shape or form is good for our mental, physical and spiritual health. Yoga has been practised for 1000's of years for good reason. Regular yoga practice can reduce blood pressure, heartrate, and can even help depression and anxiety. It's the most gentle type of exercise you can do and is perfect for all ages. Apart from being more flexible and happier, I find it simply helps me to breathe better. Rarely do any of us take the time to do belly breathing* and that means we are all lacking in oxygen. Yoga helps you to focus on your breath and allows you to breathe a lot more deeply. No-one is expecting you to perform complex headstands in the sea, it's good to start with something simple and you can do as much or as little as you like to begin with. You can try and find a yoga class in your local area but as you should be doing a small amount each day I advise you to buy a DVD called 'Yoga for Dummies'. The DVD has a few different practises on it OR if you want to keep it cheap and simple, the sequence that will be most beneficial to you to learn can be found on YouTube under 'Yoga for Dummies, The Daily Dozen'. The sequence takes about an hour to do when you begin, however once you have learnt the 12 steps it will only take about 20 minutes to do the practice everyday and you will start to notice by week 3 quite a few improvements to your mind, body and soul.

The way to practice belly breathing is to place your hand onto your stomach and take a deep breath in. Your stomach should rise on the in breath and fall as you breath out. Practice this and make sure this is how you breathe when doing your yoga.

NO DRAMA

As we are focusing on our frequency in week 2, it's important to try and do all that you can to keep your frequency as high as possible. As amazingly easy as it is to feel happy in our own little bubble, for some of us it often doesn't take much for someone we know to come and cloud us with their negativity and instantly wash away all of our happiness. We all know those types of people that just suck the life out of you. These people are called 'energy vampires' and they will absorb your energy and lower your frequency. They are so draining that you will be spiritually and mentally depleted when around them. This is NOT good for you. Remember that you don't have to answer calls from people that bring you down; you don't have to 'do' lunch or party with them; your children can play with other children; you can ask your boss to move you, there are always other options and ways to remove yourself from the situation. Some people, unfortunately even our own family at times, can be unbearable. We do not need to be mean or rude but we do not have to give them our time. These types of negative people rarely add anything of any value to our lives and it's okay to ignore them and just do you.

NO BAD VIBES

Ok, this bit is short and simple. If you have time to talk about others and their lives then yours must be perfect, right? I doubt it, so just worry about you and YOUR life. Observing other people either enviously or critically is damaging to both that person AND you. Gossiping is such a waste of time and so bad for you that you would be better off sticking pins in your eyes. What would be better would be to meet with friends and talk about each others goals and dreams and ways you could help each other achieve them. You should only worry about improving your own life. Stop judging, start loving and watch the happiness flow.....

I PROMISE MYSELF

To be so strong that nothing can disturb my peace of mind.

To talk health, happiness and prosperity to every person I meet.

To make all my friends feel that there is something worthwhile in them.

To look at the sunny side of everything and make my
optimism come true.

To think only of the best, to work only for the best
and to expect only the best.

To be just as enthusiastic about the success of others
as I am about my own.

To forget the mistakes of the past and press on to the greater
achievements of the future.

To wear a cheerful expression at all times and give a smile to
every living creature I meet.

To give so much time to improving myself that I have no time to
criticize others.

To be too large for worry, too noble for anger, too strong for fear, and too
happy to permit the presence of trouble.

To think well of myself and to proclaim this fact to the world, not in
loud words, but in great deeds.

To live in the faith that the whole world is on my side, so long as I am
true to the best that is in me.

BY
CHARLES D LARSON

WHY DID THE CHICKEN CROSS THE ROAD?

To get away from all the meat eaters *OBVIOUSLY*.

I have left this until last so you would have time to recover from the shock before week 3 kicks in. Try to remember everything in this book comes from my own research and experience and I have only put it in this book as I truly believe it will help you to be happier. It's now time to cut down (and eventually out) your consumption of all the bad white stuff; white refined flour, white refined sugar, white meat, cows milk and cheese. White refined 'anything' is bad for you but white refined sugar is one of THE most toxic things we can consume and is one of the main contributers in the epidemic of obesity and diabetes we are currently facing. Did you know dairy products are basically mucus? Technically speaking milk and cheese are animal snot and if you don't like that truth then I suggest you stop consuming them now. If you wouldn't eat your own snot, why would you eat anyone else's...especially a cow's?! Apart from the fact it is gross, when we consume products made primarily of mucus it causes us to produce more mucus and that is when disease starts to form. Children especially have a hard time with dairy products and eliminating dairy can help so many things such as common coughs and colds and skin problems such as eczema and can even help with more serious problems such as asthma. Milk goes through such a damaging process that it is nothing more than sugar and nearly void of all vitamins and nutrients after pasteurization. Dairy products encourage and increase our phlegm production and it is vital we cut down/out our intake of them. Going vegan and dairy-free is not a decision to be taken lightly but I believe it to be a vital one. However, cutting out everything and doing it too quickly can be problematic if you are not prepared. Animal and dairy products are everywhere and it will take a while to change your lifestyle but it is important you start to make this change for you health AND your happiness.You can take things slowly and start this week by cutting out all cows milk. You can switch to almond, oat or hazelnut, luckily there are so many other alternative milks to choose from! The week after you could remove cheese, the next week chicken, etc. Remember you do not have to go completely vegan instantly, but in order to achieve optimum happiness levels it is wise to follow this plan properly and to start cutting out these harmful products.

For as long as men massacre animals, they will kill each other.
Indeed, he who sows the seed of murder and pain cannot reap joy and love.

PYTHAGORAS

THE HAPPY DIET WEEK 2 SUMMARY:

- Start yoga or some sort of exercise daily. (Yoga is preferable and the most beneficial)

- Start removing yourself from toxic people and stop gossiping/worrying about others. Worry ONLY about yourself and speak ONLY of positive things.

- Start cutting out/down all white refined flour and sugar, white meat and dairy products.

- Watch a documentary called 'Earthlings' (you won't be happy when you watch it but you will understand why meat is so bad for us and how it is destroying our planet. Knowledge is power and you can only be happy when you truly understand what is keeping you UNhappy.)

Added Happy:

Chia seeds are a great way to help keep you alert and awake all day. They are a protein packed, vitamin dense, fibre rich super food and adding a teaspoon of pre-soaked chia seeds to whatever you have in the morning will make a huge difference to your energy levels later on in the day.
Method: Add a teaspoon (or 2) to a glass, cover with water an allow to sit for 10-15 mins. Soon you will see them turn into what looks like frog spawn (don't be alarmed this is normal). Next add them to either your breakfast smoothie/juice or if you're brave and you can stand the texture, add them to your morning water.

THE HAPPY DIET

....

"people, even more than things, have to be restored, renewed, revived, reclaimed and redeemed. never throw out anyone."

AUDREY HEPBURN

BYE BYE BAD VIBES, HELLLOOOO HAPPINESS.....

In week 3 we are taking a more spiritual approach on our path to happiness. We are going to be looking at dissolving the negative energy we may be storing in us from past bad experiences and turning it into something positive. We are going to work to release the past, start looking forward to a better future and most importantly we will work on being happy in the present.

LET IT GO

We all at some point have experienced something that leaves us with an emotional scar. It's those scars that are the most damaging to our energy and have the biggest effect on our lives. To help to heal these scars, I am going to ask you to perform the following exercise:

THE RELEASE TECHNIQUE:

1. THE LIST

I want you to think about all the things that have hurt you in your life. The things that still upset you, no matter when they happened or if something is happening now. I want you to write all of it down in a list. When that list is finished (keep this safe) I want you to pick the 3 most painful things on that list and write each out on a seperate piece of paper. Ponder on this list for a few days if you must, as it is important you get all your pain, both past and present into this list. Keep the list and the 3 pieces of paper safe.

2. THE STONES

Next go for a walk and find some small stones. If for some reason you cannot get outside or can't find stones then you can use bits of Lego, grapes or small coins, whatever it is does not matter, just find 3 smallish objects you can stand to lose and keep them safe.

3. FILLING UP THE STONES

You need to make sure you are somewhere that you feel safe and relaxed. You do not want to be disturbed and this step ideally needs to be performed outdoors. The natural elements can lend silent support when doing something like this, so it is quite important you try to do this somewhere quietly outside. However if you are unable to get out then privately in your bedroom will do. Next you need to take one of the pieces of paper with your pain on and wrap it tightly around the stone or object. Here is where I want you to take a moment to hold that stone. For a minute or two stare at the stone and then close your eyes, wrap your left hand tightly around it and FEEL your pain pouring from you into that stone. Imagine the stone is a sponge that absorbs sadness, put all of your sadness and hurt into that stone and ask the stone to help take away your pain. Next, ask the universe to help you move forward. Put the stone wrapped in paper aside. Then Repeat the process again for the remaining 2 stones. I must stress for this to work you really need to imagine and actually feel the negative energy leaving your body and transferring into the stone. Imagine the thing that brings sadness, that sadness-that tightening you feel in your chest and your tummy, breathe it out, literally feel yourself blowing it all into the stones. It is very important to do this, because as wacko as this sounds that tight sad feeling is an energy block and you need to remove it from yourself in order to be able to move forward into a happier existence.

4. RELEASING

Now you should be left with three wrapped up stones and a list. For the next part of this you definitely need to be outside and you will also need a lighter. There's a lot to be said about the cleansing elements nature has to offer. If you can get yourself to somewhere there is water then that would be perfect; the sea, a river, pond, lake or if you can't get to anything like that then do it in your garden or the park. Take a moment to hold your stones (in your left hand) and, again, really feel the last of that painful energy leave you and go into those stones. Then tell yourself that once these stones have gone, so has the negative energy and with it the pain will go too. Ask the universe to help you move forward and be thankful for the help to do this, you may want to say something like the following:

"I fully and completely release the past. I now choose to move forward with my life. I choose to live in love. Please deliver me all the goodness that is mine by divine right and allow me to live a wonderful existence from this day forward."

Then with everything you have throw those stones as far as you possibly can. And I mean as far as you can.

When you throw those stones, the negative energy that has been stored up inside you and holding you back from living the best life you can will go with them too. Throw those stones and when they are gone so is your past and your problems. Next, set fire to that list and watch the rest of your problems burn away. Just let go of all the other things.

MOVING FORWARD

You deserve more than a life filled with unhealed pain and you can choose now to heal it and let it go. All us humans have choices in life. We choose to get up and go to work. We choose the job that we do. We choose how we raise our children. But one of the most important choices we will ever make is how we choose to live our life. Carrying past trauma and allowing it to stop us from being happy is a choice and today it is about making a choice to let it go. You can choose to stay living in the past and hold on to that negative energy or you can do the exercise, brush your shoulders off and decide to move forward with your life into a better existence. You can choose a better outcome. You can choose to be happy.

DON'T HATE, MEDITATE.

When we hear someone say "I meditate", we tend to have visions of a 100+ year old yogi sitting on top of a mountain in India chanting 'Om'. However times are different and now mediation is something that is respected and practiced globally. Meditation is not only a useful manifestation tool, it is also a great way to relax and unwind and it is actually proven to make you happier! Just 15 minutes of meditation a day can reduce stress levels significantly and increase productivity in phenomenal amounts.

GUIDED MEDITATION

Perform the following in a quiet space every evening in weeks 3+4 for approximately 15 minutes. This meditation is best to perform after doing yoga:

- Find a warm, quiet space and light a candle. Make sure you won't be interrupted.

- Sit cross legged, supporting your back if you need to.

- Begin by taking a very long, very deep breath in through your nose. Make sure the air goes into your stomach and not your chest. (Breathing into your stomach instead of your chest is called belly breathing and is how we should all breathe. You may need to spend some time practicing this as most of us breathe from our chests, but take some time and make sure your stomach is filling up when breathing in.)

- Breathe out through your nose, again slowly. You want to hear a sort of ocean air noise as you breathe. Repeat 3 times.

- As you breathe out, imagine you are breathing out anything negative in you. Any stresses you have just blow them away and feel them leave your body every-time you breathe out*.

- Keep breathing and try to imagine a violet light pouring down from above and into the top of your head and imagine your self over flowing with love and happiness.

- Any thoughts you have, acknowledge them and let them pass, do not dwell on them.

- Once you truly stop observing your thoughts, you will start feeling very floaty and detached (this may take days/weeks/months to properly achieve so do not worry).

- Enjoy this place of calm and just breathe and bathe in the love of the universe.

- When you feel ready, slowly open your eyes and start to focus back on this world.

- Doing this everyday will rapidly improve your happiness levels.

Please be mindful that some of the energy you are releasing could be harmful and can easily transfer into other people and things. Try to aim it somewhere that can handle it. I find that out of the window and into the wind is the best place to direct it.

BE PROUD OF YOURSELF!

The last thing you must do this week is go and find a mirror. When you get there, take a good long look at yourself and say to yourself LOUDLY 'I am amazing and I love every bit of me!' Then fling your arms around yourself and give yourself a big fat hug. You have made it this far and quite frankly you are freakin' fantastic. What you have done up to this point and the amount you have achieved is INCREDIBLE! Maybe go and check that mirror again, as you might have started to sprout some sort of angel wings as you truly are wonderful to have got here. Well done!

THE HAPPY DIET WEEK 3 SUMMARY

· Continue to maintain the practices of weeks 1+2

· Do the release exercise

· Meditate for at least 15 mins either after yoga or at the end of every-day

· Get in the mirror and tell yourself how much you love YOU!

ADDED HAPPY:

Affirmations are a great way of helping to change habits and be happier. Think of some positive things you can say, such as ' I love and accept every piece of my amazing self, thank you universe for my happiness and my health!' You can say them out loud or in your head, but try and remember to say them three times in a row, 3x a day. You will be pleasantly surprised at the power of this!

· ·

(Fill in the blank, hint: you can
be *ANYTHING* you want to be)

week 4
THE HAPPY DIET

....

"happiness is not something ready made, it comes from your own actions."

DALAI LAMA XIV

At this point you have elevated your frequency by forming new positive habits in both your living, eating and exercising regimes and your energy is now flowing. You should be feeling amazing and in week four you are going to learn how to really elevate and 'seal in' your happiness.

ALL THINGS ARE GREAT, NO MATTER HOW SMALL

We know happiness is not a particular 'thing'. We know it is a state of mind and the more things we can do to induce that state, the better. How do we do this? Quite simply we must learn to find joy in all things great, *especially* the small. Sometimes do something smple, like stop and stare at a patch of wild flowers and admire the way they grow so effortlessly. Smell their amazing scent and think how grateful you are for the flowers AND your nose. Imagine if you couldn't smell anything, you would soon be more happy to experience a simple thing such as smelling a flower. Look up at the sun that gives us life and be grateful for it's rays. Be happy again because you have healthy eyes to see the sun and the stars with. All the material things the media tries to convince us we need to be happy, we actually really don't. I do believe we should all be wealthy BUT not to the detriment of our own health or our society. Whether you are the richest or poorest human alive, we all have the same sun and stars to look at and they are where the magic is. Take joy in the cleansing wind and the purifying rain, be deeply grateful for it. Sit quietly and take time to taste all the flavours of the food you have to eat, bless your food and give thanks for it. Do you know how many people didn't eat today? Do you know how many people didn't wake up today? Do you know how many won't tomorrow? You are so blessed to be here and if you are reading this book in a safe house with a fridge even half full of food, that puts you in the top 10% of the luckiest people in the world and it's good to realise that. Whatever you may have be it great or small, start to bless it and not only will you see it multiply, your quality of life will greatly improve.

GRATITUDE DIARY

In this final week I want you to start writing a daily gratitude journal. If you want you can buy a special notebook or you can just use scrap paper, where and what you write it on does not matter, but write it you must. Being grateful helps us to see where our lives shine and show us just how much we are blessed. Gratitude also helps us to live in the now and be mindful of what we have. However, I believe the best part of gratitude is the universe's insistence on giving us more things to be grateful for once we really start practising gratitude and being thankful. There is something about gratitude that the universe loves and it speeds joy to all those who practice it.

Every night after meditation, sit for about 5 minutes and write down at least 2-3 things you are grateful for that day. Just spend a few minutes really feeling grateful from your heart and giving thanks to the universe for whatever it is you are grateful for. Try and find new things to be thankful for everyday. In all the books I have read on success and happiness they all say to be grateful in all that you do and for all that you have. I personally start and finish everyday saying a big list of 'thank you's' and really FEEL it in my heart. As soon as I wake I start thanking, I say 'thank you' for waking up to another day; 'thank you' that I have eyes to open; 'thank you' for the bed I just slept in; 'thank you' for the shower I am about to have, and I go on and on and on. Scientists are now starting to confirm what philosophers and mystics have said for years, that gratitude is good for your health and can improve our life in so many ways. Switch your attitude to gratitude!

DO SOMETHING FOR SOMEONE ELSE

As crazy as it sounds doing things to make OTHER people happy is actually the fastest way to achieve your own happiness. That warm fuzzy feeling you get when you make someone else smile will stay with you for a long time, believe me. We spend a lot of time working to buy things that are not even really valuable. I'm not saying you can't buy happiness as you most certainly can, but it's what you are buying that matters. For instance, if you are hungry and you go to a restaurant or buy a takeaway you are satisfying that need and making yourself momentarily happy even though you probably have food in the fridge at home. BUT, if someone is hungry and cannot afford to eat and you are able to help them by providing a meal, the pure joy and happiness you will get from being able to provide this happiness to others will have you feeling like you are walking on sunshine. This happiness will last longer than any takeaway for yourself and is so fulfilling for the human spirit. There is an ancient Chinese proverb that says:

If you want happiness for an hour, take a nap.
If you want happiness for a day, go fishing.
If you want happiness for a month, get married.
If you want happiness for a year, inherit a fortune.
If you want happiness for a lifetime, help somebody else.

So whether you buy a homeless person lunch or volunteer at your local soup kitchen once a month, do something to start spreading love to others and the love will be returned 10 fold, I promise.

DO SOMETHING FOR YOU

Finally, I'm a big believer in occasionally being a bit selfish and just doing something for YOU. We as individuals are so important but, in the grand scheme of life we can sometimes get lost. It is so vital we take good care of ourselves, especially if you have young children or a stressful job. Sometimes that means being selfish and shutting off from the world and getting some 'me time'. Go and have a massage or a facial; go and read a book in the park; take a walk, maybe go and meet some new people. Whatever you do just make sure it's what YOU want and it's making YOU happy. Try and indulge yourself at least once a month and set aside a few hours just for you. It's good to have something to look forward to and loving ourselves is a huge part of maintaining our own happiness.

Kindness is free, sprinkle that shit everywhere.

NOT DR. TAMARA

THE HAPPY DIET WEEK 4 SUMMARY

• Continue to maintain the practises of weeks 1, 2 + 3

• Write down at LEAST three things every day that you are grateful for in a gratitude journal or notebook

• Either volunteer or do something genuinely nice for someone else regularly

• Treat yourself to something that is just for you at least once a month

ADDED HAPPY:

After you have written down what you are grateful for, sit for a minute and really FEEL the gratitude. Try and feel the warmth and loving energy pouring out of your heart. When you say the words 'Thank You', you should say them from your heart sincerely and feel as though that's where they are coming from. This will super charge your words of thanks and really help to change your life for the better.

<u>YOU HAVE MADE IT!!!</u>

You have finally finished The Happy Diet and if you are not feeling happier yet, I will eat my own book! You have done amazingly well to get this far and I and the universe congratulate you on being so absolutely wonderful. You are finally at the end of a massive shift and four weeks of changing and growing for the better and you should be glowing with pride. These changes to your diet, exercise regime and attitude are all going to help you live a more naturally happy life if you continue with them. I am so proud of you for getting this far, I truly am. All of the advice I have given in this book I believe, is vital for a happy existence and that is all I wish for each and every one of you, true happiness. You should feel lighter, more energetic and ready to take on the world. Use this new energy wisely and spread your light everywhere you go. The universe needs happy people and just by waking up and choosing to smile you have already helped to save a bit of the world. Thank YOU,

You are Amazing

The End.

(although technically, this is just the beginning)